THE
Last Time
I'LL
Write About
You

Also by Dawn Lanuza

THE Last Time I'LL Write About You

DAWN LANUZA

Andrews McMeel
PUBLISHING®

Andrews McMeel Publishing
a division of Andrews McMeel Universal
1130 Walnut Street, Kansas City, Missouri 64106

www.andrewsmcmeel.com
www.dawnlanuza.com

21 22 23 24 25 BVG 10 9 8 7 6 5 4

ISBN: 978-1-4494-9318-9

Edited by Layla Tanjutco
Cover design by Reginald Lapid (society6.com/reglapid)
Illustrations by Luntian Dumlao (instagram.com/luntiandumlao)

Library of Congress Control Number: 2017951835

Editor: Patty Rice
Art Director: Holly Swayne
Production Editor: Elizabeth A. Garcia
Production Manager: Cliff Koehler

ATTENTION: SCHOOLS AND BUSINESSES
Andrews McMeel books are available at quantity discounts with bulk
purchase for educational, business, or sales promotional use. For information,
please e-mail the Andrews McMeel Publishing Special Sales Department:
specialsales@amuniversal.com.

To young hearts,
Keep beating.
Keep breaking.
Keep falling in love.

THE FIRST

SUNBEAM

You light up the room
Wherever you go
With your wit and charm
You turn things around.

You light up the room
You're a rush of blood
You're a ray of sun
You lighten me up.

THE OBJECT OF MY

I love the way you look
Your eyes, they twinkle
Your lips, they curl
Your whole spirit lifts.

I love the way you look
As I watch you across the room
That is until you looked at me
And nothing else could compare.

✦WHAT I LIKE ABOUT YOU✦

Your hand
    How you held the small of my back
Your fingers
    How they grasped mine as we crossed the street
Your feet
    How they led us to your room
The chain on your neck
    How it slid through my fingers as I pulled you in
Your eyes
    How they spoke to me
Your bed
    How it welcomed us both
Your lips
    Oh, how they silenced my doubts

You are the dream
But I've had wake-up calls

IN A NUTSHELL

I'm not brave enough to love you
The same way
You're not strong enough to take me on.

"He was good for you."
"I don't doubt it."

"Then why'd you let him go?"

"I wasn't good for him."

BOTTOM LINE

This is how it's going to be:
A million unanswered questions,
A thousand books you'd never ask me to read,
A hundred movies we'd never fall asleep in together,
A couple of songs I won't hear you sing in the shower,
A few words I would never interrupt with a kiss,
A piece of you, I'll miss every single day.

This is how it's going to be.
I should be alright with that.

TRUTH

You read these things
And you ask the world,
Why doesn't it happen
To someone like you?

Deep in your heart,
You know the answer:
It's because you don't let it.

AND NOW I'M RUINED

When I met you
I always wondered
How I'd never met
Anyone quite like you

When we parted
I always wondered
How everyone else
Reminded me of you

DECOY

You're not it

Although you filled in that spot quite convincingly.

You're not it

Can you get up from that seat so we can move along accordingly?

★CONSPIRACY THEORY★

We always had our thing
Even when we were fighting
We were allies,
Partners in crime
We built each other's walls up
To keep others out.

THE PULL

CONFESSION

I told everyone
I love you
Sorry if they knew before you

To be fair,
I think everyone knew
Before I did, too.

CONSISTENCY

I don't think you think of me
The way I think of you
For you do so only sporadically
While I have you in me
Constantly.

HEAD COUNT

How many of us
Have slept in your bed
Which one did you intend to keep

How many of us
Held up your head
While you continued to sleep

How many of us
Believed the promises you made
How many did you let weep

REASONS FOR REJECTION

I hope you know
I said no
Not because I didn't want to

I knew better than to rush it
We always seem to fall
Into each other too easily

So much so that when we part
It's like Velcro
Gone, in a blink of an eye

Painless then
But the sound lingers
Then haunts

I hope you know
I want more
Than that day stretched into hours

I want you every day
Kissing me good night
Til tomorrow
And tomorrow
And tomorrow
And tomorrow
And tomorrow
And tomorrow.

MIGRATORY BIRDS

I watched you move
From girl to girl
Or has it always been
You, moving on from her
With me
To another

Has it always been
Me, watching you
Never quite knowing
How to be with yourself?

HH

You're the face of innocence,
Of sunny days,
Long and leisurely walks
And happy talks.

I liked remembering you this way.

You're the face of change,
Of late nights,
Beer bottles, ashtrays
And ignored calls.

You broke my heart this way.

You're the face of my youth,
Of second and too many chances,
Two clasped hands
At the back of the car.

I wish we could have just stayed.

THE NTH BREAKFAST

Hot coffee
Burnt tongue
Confiding exclusively
Of woes unsung

Warm hands
Kind smile
Eyes seeking to understand—
But you lie.

✦METAMORPHOSIS✦

for Anton

I built a cocoon made of stories of you.
I intend to stay with your memories
Where it's warm and good.

I built a cocoon made of stories of you.
But one day,
I'll have to break through.

✗HABITS✗

A lot of things changed between us
Like how I used to hate breakfast
And how you'd always insist

Now I'm craving pancakes
Coffee, bacon
Even at odd hours of the day

Meanwhile you've learned
To stop asking these things
And cared less if I've missed a meal

A lot of things changed between us
Like how I cared after you left,
And how you just didn't.

PEACE TALKS

You realize
This war could end
If we could just
Whisper the words,
I'm sorry
As our lips crash?
Catch the pain
I'll take yours
Here, take mine
Back and forth.

Let's communicate
With teeth and lips and tongue.

THE KISS

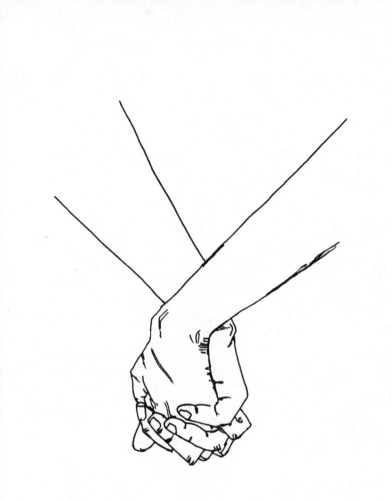

RATIONALE

All this time you've been trying
To undress me
From head to toe

All this time I've insisted
That I've got scars
Underneath it all

All this time that you don't have anymore
All these fears that I've kept close

Yet

All this time, I've been unraveling
With all these hopes that you're still watching

I doubt it.
But here you go.

✶6 A.M.✶

Waking up is never the same
Not without your arms tangled up in mine
Not without your kiss on my cheek
Not without you telling me,
"You look beautiful today."

✗OTHER MEANS OF COMMUNICATION ✗

I like how our hands seem to have their own
conversations, apart from our mouths.
I like how we tell things we can't seem to say out loud.
In these spaces between,
Our fingers meet,
And they fit.
Perfectly.
There are no walls.
No secrets.

I like how our hands know how to be together
At times we can't seem to.

RESOLVE

I could keep saying
One more
Just one more
But when does it end?

REFLECTION

The thing is,
I used to remember your laugh.
I hear it behind my ear,
It tickles me.

I feel your breath.
I sense your nerves.
I keep this memory of you
For the longest time.

Now that I've forgotten
I tried to remember.
Trust me,
I'm the only one left trying to remember.

What it's like to have you near
That I can feel your breath
The tremble in your voice
As it creates waves in me

Stirring,
Kneading,
Making me faint.

This is all imaginary
For I can no longer remember.
I am only creating the memory.

This is no longer you.
This is all me.

★NORTHERN STAR★

Look up at the sky
Like once upon a time
Look up and I
Will guide you back to me.

I meant to keep you
But I didn't want to be kept
See the problem?

MODERN VAMPIRES

The sun burns my skin
In your bed as we lay
It's a clear sign:
We're not made for the day.

We're creatures of the night
Straddled in the sheets
The dawn is in sight
We part as soon as we meet.

GRIM, NOT A FAIRY TALE

He's no hero
He's the villain
She took all the blame;
He skillfully played the game.

He's no prince
She's learned since
Now she wears armor for skin
And keeps her heart closed in.

THE TALK

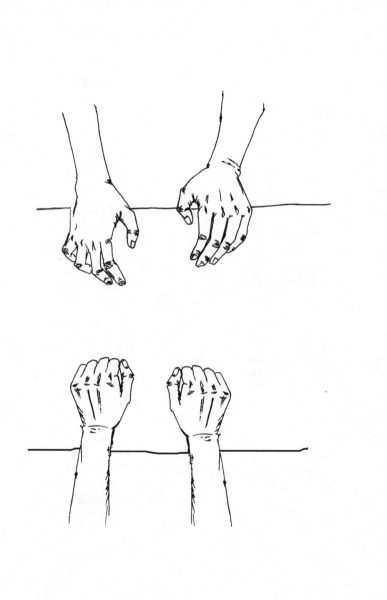

★SUSTENANCE★

When I think about you in huge doses,
I drown.
In despair,
In longing,
In guilt.

I learned to think of you
In tiny rations
Like meals delivered to my plate
Three times a day

Each time enough
To nourish me,
To make me hope,
To keep my heart alive.

THE WORST SLEEPOVER

Is there anything stranger
Than sleeping on the same bed
With a man who has changed?

Not in who he was,
But in the way that
He has looked at you.

A week ago he promised
This time, he'll stay
But his eyes are worlds away

You held on to him
In that forsaken bed
He's distant, cold—

Nothing else could be said.

ARE YOU OKAY?
I'm shouting this to the universe
In case you needed to answer.

THE FEAR

I used to thank you
For making me feel beautiful
And you assured me,
I am.

Since you left
All I've felt is horrible
And I'm so scared you realized,
I am.

OUR SONG

That one morning
You told me,
"To the ends of the Earth."
Nothing more.

You were quoting that song
So I didn't say anything
But I keep going back to that
Now that we are on polar opposites.

Intentionally or not
We've drifted apart
But I keep holding on to that
Like a promise.

Cause I still think of you
While I'm safely tucked here
Hoping I could reach out
To where you've run away.

UNASKED QUESTION

Was I a secret not worth sharing
Or
Was I a fact not worth telling?

REVOLVING DOOR

Maybe you wanted me to hate you
Cause God knows I love you
Maybe you hate me too
Cause why else would you
Walk in and out of my life
Like you were in a revolving door?

I watch you at it
Spinning and spinning
I wait for you to decide,
To stop,
Look at me,
Come inside.

Stay?

Maybe you wanted me to hate you
Forget that I love you
So I can stop watching
And you can stop spinning
Cause God knows it's exhausting
To be inside that revolving door.

And maybe
Just maybe
That's why you hate me
Cause it was just you spinning
As it always has been
In that revolving door.

HERE'S LOOKING AT YOU, KID

Don't tell me I can't get over it
You stood by my window that night
And waited for me to come out

Don't
You
Dare
Put
This
All
On
Me

You loved me just as much
In fact
You loved me too much

The only difference is that
You loved me when I didn't care enough
And I loved you when you stopped.

NO APOLOGIES

I wasn't ready
You thought I wasn't willing
I told you I'm sorry
You just stopped believing.

LIKE A GREEK TRAGEDY

Suits me to start falling
I've always loved reading tragedies
I just didn't think you'd be
In one of these sad stories.

WE'RE NOT BEGGARS

I told you not to love so much
I hope you did not listen
It's better that you do it all out
Than hand out scraps
To people who truly need it.

RESUSCITATE

You keep coming back to him
To convince yourself that
You still feel,
You still hurt,
Your heart still works.

But that's not love,
Don't hang on to that.

✘NOTICE OF EVICTION✘

You need to move out
Pick up your stuff,
Dust the corners of my heart.

You need to move out
Sweep the floor,
Take your writings off the wall.

You need to move out
Clear out the space,
Leave absolutely no trace.

You need to move out
So my quiescent heart
Learns to love again.

THE HURT

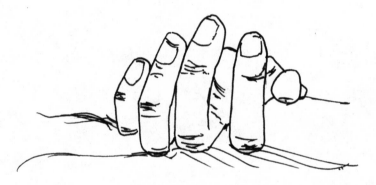

MEMENTO

Throughout the years we've kept:
Tickets to concerts
Stubs from movies
Prize toys from cereal boxes
Notes scribbled
Books swapped
CDs burned

I don't know what we were thinking.
Now that we're apart
I have all of your stuff.

I asked you, *should I return it?*
You said, *hold on to it.*
Then added,
It's a reason for us to see each other again.

The last time we talked
We mentioned these mementos—
Things that were not ours but in our possession.

I lost your book, you said.
I have your favorite movie, I claimed.
Keep it, you concluded.

Somehow keeping it
Wasn't as comforting
As holding on to it
So we can see each other again.

When did we become such a bad idea?

THE MENTOR

Teach me how to forget
Like how you taught me your name
These words, what they meant
And which one you liked best.

Teach me how to forget
Like how you taught me to say
Good morning, good night,
Every damn day of our lives.

Teach me how to forget
Like how you taught me your secrets
Silly jokes, careful confessions
Anecdotes and one-liners.

Teach me how to forget
Like how you taught me to believe
How easy it was to disappear
Over

And
Over
Until I can no longer remember
The last time you were there.

IN HINDSIGHT

Darkness is a friend
We've been long acquainted
It was nice knowing your light
But I couldn't be mended.

Sadness is a cloak
I wear around my shoulders
You let the sun soak
On my skin to recover.

But the dark, it remains
And you were slowly fading
You bring the sun,
But it keeps on setting.

THE PENSIEVE

I would like to see me in your memory
Maybe then I'd understand
How we turned out to be
From the very best
To this colossal mess

PLEA

You can't help
Those who don't want to be helped
That's what you said,
I heard it.

I can't help
How I felt
This is how I bled
You didn't see it.

I liked you so much that I even dated your friends.

MEMORY

Did you ever talk about me
The way I talked about you?
With a smile or a sigh
Never a frown or a curse.

Did I leave you enough memories?
I bleed your impressions
Your every laugh and musing,
Your stories and dreams.

ROOT

It's funny how
The thought of you makes me mad
When all along I thought
You're the one person I'd exclude from that.

That was the problem:
I rooted for you.
And you?
You were just being you.

I expected you to spare me
Of any hurt,
Of any lie,
Thinking I deserved it.

Sometimes
I think this hate
Is not because you hurt me
Or because you lied.

You proved me wrong
And that stings more
Than all of the things
You've done combined.

How many times do I have to break my heart
before I get it right?

IN CASE OF EMERGENCY,
PLEASE ACT ACCORDINGLY

I hope I never see you again
      (But if I do)
Let's not speak of this,
Let it be our little secret.

But if I do
      (Because I will)
I hope I get to tell you,
Hello
And mean it when I say,
Goodbye.

DRUNK DIALING GHOSTS

I never drink
But when I do,
Sometimes I call you.
It would have been shitty
Except the phone never rings.

I never drink
But when I do,
I keep forgetting
That you never again told me
How to reach you.

I guess I'm just gonna live with you living inside my head.

MYSTERY SOLVED

I think you loved me
And I loved you
But we never really did

At the same time.

CAUTION

I tell myself,
Stop stepping on broken glass
But it's too late for that.
You can't break what's already been torn apart.

ANALOGY

You gave me a box of paint
I never used it
Much like
You came to me with so much
And I refused it.

P.S. I still have the box. I wrote your name on it, in case
someone dared to take it from me.

FRAGILE, HANDLE WITH CARE

I kept your clothes
In case you're wondering
They're in a box labeled *yours*
Mixed with the things we've been missing

THE LAST

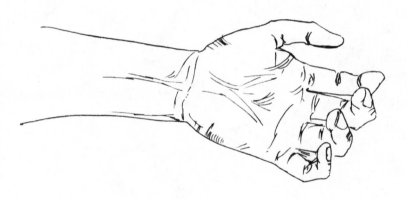

Should I be
Thankful
Or
Regretful
That my only idea
Of love
Is
You?

FOREIGN BEDS

Late night
In strange places
And foreign beds
I find myself thinking of you
Where you are
How you've been
Who you're with that very second

I don't ask
For these are simple questions
Only asked by people who matter
Your family,
Your friends,
Your lover.

No longer
Never will be
Me.

BOTH FEET ON SHORE

You're not coming back, are you?
I got used to having you drop by
Every once in a while
That I've convinced myself
That you were coming home

As if you belong with me,
Not out on the sea.

✷ECHOES✷

Your words
Stuck to my skin
Painted all over
Tattooed well under

Your words
Scarce over the years
Stuck to my head
Played back like a record

I wish I could tell you
All I didn't say then
I wish I could give you
Answers you were searching
I wish you were here,
I wish you were still near.

Your words
Faint as a whisper
Stick to me, still
Cause it's all I have left

Of what we have and what could have been.

STILL

My favorite part of waking up at night
Is realizing that you're holding me
That somehow, our subconscious
Found a way to keep us linked:

Arms around my waist
Thighs interlaced
Foreheads leaning in
Our breaths colliding

It's so quiet,
So calm,
So tranquil,
That I drift off with a grin.

I wake up at night sometimes
Still
Sometimes from a bad dream
Sometimes for no reason at all

Then I feel sorry
For you're no longer there
To wrap me in your arms
And kiss the nightmares away.

★THE WORLD IS OUR SOUVENIR★

The world remembers
What we try to forget
It's in the embers
Of the things we left

It's in the concrete,
The streets we used to tread
In the halls we used to meet
When we had hours to spend

It's in the book you carried home
In this umbrella we shared
It's in the stars you wished on
In your skin, your palms,
Your fingers: playing with my hair

It's in your unmade bed
The wrinkle, the weight
It's in the distance to the door I traveled
In the silence, partings unsaid.

LESSON

I'm tired of missing you
So I made a point to forget you
But it gets exhausting
Once you learn:
Forgetting is just another form of remembering.

CROOKED

I always felt like
Begging for your forgiveness
For the things I was afraid of
For the things you couldn't fix

But I realized
I never owed you anything
I never needed your approval
I just needed to forgive myself

I found myself, bent:
Never quite broken,
Never quite lost,
Never quite yours.

I just want to stop wasting the time I've been wasting on you.

THE LAST STRAND

I don't even know you
I mean
I used to
But you've become this nameless face.

You tried my patience
Tugged on the rope,
Yanked and pulled
Until you reached the point.

I don't even know you.
I mean,
I really used to.
Sometimes I still wish I do

But I can only take so much
And you had the last strand.

You can't hurt me anymore.

Not that you should try.
Not that I should let you.

FULL CIRCLE

I told you once,
Maybe someday I'll write about you.
You asked me not to,
Said you wouldn't read it.

You came to me
A few days ago
Told me you'd read my work,
Come back to me with what you thought.

Days passed and you never did
And I get it:

I lied;
You didn't.

AURORA

You can keep ignoring me
But I will not live in the shadows
I am here,
I am light.
I am the tale you refused to tell.

I will not be silent.

ACCEPTANCE

I caught a glimpse of you
And I thought, *I love you*
Still—after all the years of
I'm over you

Maybe loving you
Will never go away
But it's over
I know, I know, I know

It is neither here
Nor there
It is a peaceful middle
And I am okay.

✘EPILOGUE✘

Despite everything
I still thank the universe
For blessing me with you
As my first

If I could love you this much
For this long
—And on my first try—
Then surely,

I could love someone else more
Far better,
Far longer.

P.S.

Think of it as cruel
Think of it as hateful
None of this is true
Believe it or not at all

This started out for you
Only it ended for me
So with finality:
This is the last time I'll ever write about you.

ABOUT THE AUTHOR

Dawn Lanuza writes contemporary romance and young adult fiction. This is her first poetry collection. She has two first loves—music and writing—and is lucky enough to surround herself with them. She works for music by day and writes meet-cutes and snappy comebacks by night.

She currently lives with her adopted cream toy poodle.

Contact her at:
www.dawnlanuza.com
dawn.lanuza@gmail.com
www.facebook.com/AuthorDawnLanuza
Twitter: @dawnlanuza

with love & gratitude to:

#romanceclass, for the support you've given to this one.
Layla Tanjutco
Mina V. Esguerra
Samantha Sotto
Reginald Lapid
Lulu Dumlao
Jay E. Tria
Mau Patajo
Patty Rice and the rest of the team at Andrews McMeel
Publishing, for taking a chance on a girl who lives halfway
around the world.
Maan and Ilia, for being on this journey with me.
My family: my mom, my sister, my brother, and my niece.
My dog.
Wonderful friends, fellow poets, authors, and lyricists—
you are the real inspiration.
Lastly, for you,
for choosing this book.

INDEX